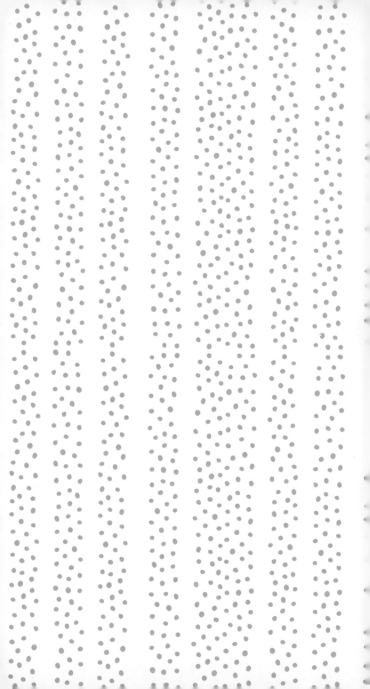

PERSONAL INFORMATION

Name:

Address:

Telephone: Email:

Employer:

Address:

Telephone: Email:

MEDICAL INFORMATION

Physician: Telephone:

Allergies:

Medications:

Blood Type:

Insurer:

IN CASE OF EMERGENCY, NOTIFY

Name:

Address:

Telephone: Relationship:

Published by DayMaker, an imprint of Barbour Publishing, Inc., 1810 Barbour Drive, Uhrichsville, Ohio 44683, www.barbourbooks.com

Our mission is to inspire the world with the life-changing message of the Bible.

Member of the
Evangelical Christian
Publishers Association

Printed in China.

Inspiration for a LESS STRESSED Life

2021 PLANNER

DAYMAKER™
An Imprint of Barbour Publishing, Inc.

Stress Less!

*Make sure that you don't get so absorbed
and exhausted in taking care of all your day-by-day
obligations that you lose track of the time and doze
off, oblivious to God. . . . Be up and awake to
what God is doing! God is putting the
finishing touches on the salvation work
he began when we first believed.*

ROMANS 13:11 MSG

No doubt about it, those much longed for peaceful moments are few and far between during our stress-filled, busy days.

Take a minute to revive and refresh your stressed-out soul with this practical planner featuring monthly devotional readings and weekly inspiration designed to encourage you to live in God's freedom. With your focus on Him, you'll find the path to a less stressed life every day of the calendar year!

YEAR at a GLANCE

JANUARY

S	M	T	W	T	F	S
					1	2
3	4	5	6	7	8	9
10	11	12	13	14	15	16
17	18	19	20	21	22	23
24	25	26	27	28	29	30
31						

FEBRUARY

S	M	T	W	T	F	S
	1	2	3	4	5	6
7	8	9	10	11	12	13
14	15	16	17	18	19	20
21	22	23	24	25	26	27
28						

MAY

S	M	T	W	T	F	S
						1
2	3	4	5	6	7	8
9	10	11	12	13	14	15
16	17	18	19	20	21	22
23	24	25	26	27	28	29
30	31					

JUNE

S	M	T	W	T	F	S
		1	2	3	4	5
6	7	8	9	10	11	12
13	14	15	16	17	18	19
20	21	22	23	24	25	26
27	28	29	30			

SEPTEMBER

S	M	T	W	T	F	S
			1	2	3	4
5	6	7	8	9	10	11
12	13	14	15	16	17	18
19	20	21	22	23	24	25
26	27	28	29	30		

OCTOBER

S	M	T	W	T	F	S
					1	2
3	4	5	6	7	8	9
10	11	12	13	14	15	16
17	18	19	20	21	22	23
24	25	26	27	28	29	30
31						

2021

MARCH

S	M	T	W	T	F	S
	1	2	3	4	5	6
7	8	9	10	11	12	13
14	15	16	17	18	19	20
21	22	23	24	25	26	27
28	29	30	31			

APRIL

S	M	T	W	T	F	S
				1	2	3
4	5	6	7	8	9	10
11	12	13	14	15	16	17
18	19	20	21	22	23	24
25	26	27	28	29	30	

JULY

S	M	T	W	T	F	S
				1	2	3
4	5	6	7	8	9	10
11	12	13	14	15	16	17
18	19	20	21	22	23	24
25	26	27	28	29	30	31

AUGUST

S	M	T	W	T	F	S
1	2	3	4	5	6	7
8	9	10	11	12	13	14
15	16	17	18	19	20	21
22	23	24	25	26	27	28
29	30	31				

NOVEMBER

S	M	T	W	T	F	S
	1	2	3	4	5	6
7	8	9	10	11	12	13
14	15	16	17	18	19	20
21	22	23	24	25	26	27
28	29	30				

DECEMBER

S	M	T	W	T	F	S
			1	2	3	4
5	6	7	8	9	10	11
12	13	14	15	16	17	18
19	20	21	22	23	24	25
26	27	28	29	30	31	

AUGUST 2020

SUNDAY	MONDAY	TUESDAY	WEDNESDAY
26	27	28	29
2	3	4	5
9	10	11	12
16	17	18	19
23	24	25	26
30	31		

THURSDAY	FRIDAY	SATURDAY
30	31	1
6	7	8
13	14	15
20	21	22
27	28	29

JULY

S	M	T	W	T	F	S
			1	2	3	4
5	6	7	8	9	10	11
12	13	14	15	16	17	18
19	20	21	22	23	24	25
26	27	28	29	30	31	

SEPTEMBER

S	M	T	W	T	F	S
		1	2	3	4	5
6	7	8	9	10	11	12
13	14	15	16	17	18	19
20	21	22	23	24	25	26
27	28	29	30			

Our Avenue to Peace

Stress is nothing to be ashamed of. It's just a signal to be recognized and addressed. The problem is when we let stress take over, try to ignore it, or imagine we can handle it in our own strength.

God knew we'd have trouble in this life, that we'd find ourselves with anxiety-causing stress. But He also gave us a way out: Jesus. Our faith in Him is our avenue to an out-of-this-world peace.

Jesus is waiting. Take a deep belly breath. Exhale. Enter that secret place where He abides. Ask Him to cover you with His wings, to raise you up. To give you the word you need to hear, the peace you need to inhale.

. . . .

I'm here, Lord, limp in Your arms.
Please fill me with Your peace.

GOALS *for this* MONTH

- ☐ ....
- ☐ ....
- ☐ ....
- ☐ ....
- ☐ ....
- ☐ ....
- ☐ ....
- ☐ ....
- ☐ ....
- ☐ ....
- ☐ ....
- ☐ ....

"Let not your hearts be troubled. Believe in God; believe also in me. . . . Peace I leave with you; my peace I give to you. Not as the world gives do I give to you. Let not your hearts be troubled, neither let them be afraid."

JOHN 14:1, 27 ESV

JULY-AUGUST 2020

Know that with God on your side,
everything is and will be fine. Open up
your mind to the wisdom and insight He has
for you. Store His words in your heart.

26—SUNDAY

27—MONDAY

28—TUESDAY

29—WEDNESDAY

30—THURSDAY

31—FRIDAY

1—SATURDAY

*"Give in to God, come to terms with him
and everything will turn out just fine. Let him
tell you what to do; take his words to heart."*

JOB 22:21-22 MSG

AUGUST 2020

Fix your eyes on the Water Walker. Keep your
ears open to His Word. In so doing, you'll be
riding above the storms within and without.

2—SUNDAY

3—MONDAY

4—TUESDAY

5—WEDNESDAY

6—THURSDAY

7—FRIDAY

8—SATURDAY

Peter got out of the boat and walked on the water and came to Jesus. But when he saw the wind, he was afraid, and beginning to sink he cried out, "Lord, save me." Jesus immediately reached out his hand and took hold of him.

MATTHEW 14:29-31 ESV

AUGUST 2020

God asks you to have a heart for His message.
To stand before Him with *boldness*. To calmly listen.
When you do, you will hear His still, small
voice in the silence of your days.

9—SUNDAY

10—MONDAY

11—TUESDAY

12—WEDNESDAY

13—THURSDAY

14—FRIDAY

15—SATURDAY

A quiet voice asked, "So Elijah,
now tell me, what are you doing here?"
1 KINGS 19:13 MSG

AUGUST 2020

Replace the world's worries with God's
wisdom. Pray and memorize Bible verses
to help you stay above the fray.

16—SUNDAY

17—MONDAY

18—TUESDAY

19—WEDNESDAY

20—THURSDAY

21—FRIDAY

22—SATURDAY

"When reports come in of wars and rumored wars, keep your head and don't panic. This is routine history; this is no sign of the end."

MATTHEW 24:6 MSG

AUGUST 2020

Pray. Tell God what's happening. Ask Him
to speak. Then actually listen to what He says.
Do what He tells you to do. Pray more, stress less.

23—SUNDAY

24—MONDAY

25—TUESDAY

26—WEDNESDAY

27—THURSDAY

28—FRIDAY

29—SATURDAY

*Trust GOD from the bottom of your heart; don't try
to figure out everything on your own. Listen for GOD's
voice in everything you do, everywhere you go;
he's the one who will keep you on track.*

PROVERBS 3:5-6 MSG

SEPTEMBER 2020

SUNDAY	MONDAY	TUESDAY	WEDNESDAY
30	31	1	2
6	7 *Labor Day*	8	9
13	14	15	16
20	21	22 *First Day of Autumn*	23 *See You at the Pole*
27	28	29	30

THURSDAY	FRIDAY	SATURDAY
3	4	5
10	11	12
17	18	19
24	25	26
1	2	3

AUGUST

S	M	T	W	T	F	S
						1
2	3	4	5	6	7	8
9	10	11	12	13	14	15
16	17	18	19	20	21	22
23	24	25	26	27	28	29
30	31					

OCTOBER

S	M	T	W	T	F	S
				1	2	3
4	5	6	7	8	9	10
11	12	13	14	15	16	17
18	19	20	21	22	23	24
25	26	27	28	29	30	31

Seeking Approval

Abraham Lincoln said, "You can please some of the people all of the time, you can please all of the people some of the time, but you can't please all of the people all of the time." Yet that is exactly what we sometimes try to do. And in the process, we end up getting stressed out, because pleasing everyone is an unattainable goal. We are looking for love and approval in all the wrong places. But what's a girl to do?

Look for *God's* approval only. Don't worry what other people might say or do. It's Him you're looking to please. It's in Him you feel secure. It's He who loves you beyond measure, who has created you for a specific reason. So make Him number one in your life, seeking to live for Him alone.

. . . .

I hope to please You, Lord, in all I say, think, and do. Show me how to serve You!

GOALS *for this* MONTH

- ☐ ....
- ☐ ....
- ☐ ....
- ☐ ....
- ☐ ....
- ☐ ....
- ☐ ....
- ☐ ....
- ☐ ....
- ☐ ....
- ☐ ....
- ☐ ....
- ☐ ....

*I'm not trying to win the approval of people,
but of God. If pleasing people were my goal,
I would not be Christ's servant.*

GALATIANS 1:10 NLT

AUGUST-SEPTEMBER 2020

Jesus kept His peace. How? He went off alone and
sought His Father God. He left the crowds and went to
a deserted and desolate place. Somewhere secluded
where He could meet with God one-on-one in the
quiet of the morning hours. Follow Him.

30—SUNDAY

31—MONDAY

1—TUESDAY

2—WEDNESDAY

3—THURSDAY

4—FRIDAY

5—SATURDAY

*And rising very early in the morning,
while it was still dark, he departed and went
out to a desolate place, and there he prayed.*
MARK 1:35 ESV

SEPTEMBER 2020

God will give you all the wisdom you
need for where you are and will keep
you from tripping up on your path.

6—SUNDAY

7—MONDAY   *Labor Day*

8—TUESDAY

9—WEDNESDAY

10—THURSDAY

11—FRIDAY

12—SATURDAY

*Then Jehoshaphat said to the king
of Israel, "But first, find out what
the LORD's word is in this matter."*
1 KINGS 22:5 GW

SEPTEMBER 2020

Have faith. Know that God is with you.
He's building up your resilience, bringing out
the best in you, training you up for the next
steps as He prospers you right where you are.

13—SUNDAY

14—MONDAY

15—TUESDAY

16—WEDNESDAY

17—THURSDAY

18—FRIDAY

19—SATURDAY

When troubles of any kind come your way,
consider it an opportunity for great joy.
JAMES 1:2 NLT

SEPTEMBER 2020

Look up to what God is doing. Keep your eyes
on His heavenly prize. Know that God has a
purpose for your life and that He will brighten
up whatever darkness may come your way.

20—SUNDAY

21—MONDAY

22—TUESDAY *First Day of Autumn*

23—WEDNESDAY

....

....

....

....

24—THURSDAY

....

....

....

....

25—FRIDAY

....

....

....

....

26—SATURDAY

....

....

....

....

*I press on to reach the end of the race and
receive the heavenly prize for which God,
through Christ Jesus, is calling us.*

PHILIPPIANS 3:14 NLT

SEPTEMBER-OCTOBER 2020

God will always come through, no matter how bad things may look. He'll take care of all that's coming against you. He'll bring you out of whatever crisis you find yourself in.

27—SUNDAY

28—MONDAY

29—TUESDAY

30—WEDNESDAY

1—THURSDAY

2—FRIDAY

3—SATURDAY

*We have no might to stand against this great
company that is coming against us. We do not
know what to do, but our eyes are upon You.*

2 CHRONICLES 20:12 AMPC

OCTOBER 2020

SUNDAY	MONDAY	TUESDAY	WEDNESDAY
27	28	29	30
4	5	6	7
11	12	13	14
18	19 Columbus Day	20	21
25	26	27	28

THURSDAY	FRIDAY	SATURDAY
1	2	3
8	9	10
15	16	17
22	23	24
29	30	31 *Halloween*

SEPTEMBER

S	M	T	W	T	F	S
		1	2	3	4	5
6	7	8	9	10	11	12
13	14	15	16	17	18	19
20	21	22	23	24	25	26
27	28	29	30			

NOVEMBER

S	M	T	W	T	F	S
1	2	3	4	5	6	7
8	9	10	11	12	13	14
15	16	17	18	19	20	21
22	23	24	25	26	27	28
29	30					

Level Ground

The quaking of our worlds—inner and outer—can leave us shaken. But God provides us with solutions. He helps us to be resilient, to absorb the shocks that come our way, to hold fast under the pressure.

God's Word repeatedly tells us not to be afraid. He has blessed us with the avenue of prayer. He invites and encourages us to abide in Him, promising that when we walk in His truth, when we believe His Word with our whole heart, mind, body, and soul, we are freed from the sins that snare, the worries that stress. And in so doing, we find His love spread out before us and our feet standing on level ground (see Psalm 26:3, 12).

* * *

I find my freedom in You, Lord Jesus.

GOALS *for this* MONTH

- ☐ ....
- ☐ ....
- ☐ ....
- ☐ ....
- ☐ ....
- ☐ ....
- ☐ ....
- ☐ ....
- ☐ ....
- ☐ ....
- ☐ ....
- ☐ ....

Jesus said to those Jews who had believed in Him, If you abide in My word [hold fast to My teachings and live in accordance with them], you are truly My disciples. And you will know the Truth, and the Truth will set you free.

JOHN 8:31-32 AMPC

OCTOBER 2020

Pause. Become aware of what's going on
mentally, physically, spiritually, and emotionally.
Remind yourself that God is with you.

4—SUNDAY

....
....
....
....

5—MONDAY

....
....
....
....

6—TUESDAY

....
....
....
....

7—WEDNESDAY

8—THURSDAY

9—FRIDAY

10—SATURDAY

*[It is] the Spirit of God that made me [which
has stirred me up], and the breath of the
Almighty that gives me life [which inspires me].*
JOB 33:4 AMPC

OCTOBER 2020

If your inner dialogue is against what God would have you believe, replace it with His truth. Then choose to own and live that truth. Not just in that moment but in every moment, day after day after day.

11—SUNDAY

12—MONDAY *Columbus Day*

13—TUESDAY

14—WEDNESDAY

15—THURSDAY

16—FRIDAY

17—SATURDAY

The LORD is my light and my salvation.
Who is there to fear?
PSALM 27:1 GW

OCTOBER 2020

Sit. Listen with both ears. Choose to sit
at your Master's feet. Gift Him with those
precious moments, and He will gift you with
peace of mind, body, heart, spirit, and soul.

18—SUNDAY

19—MONDAY

20—TUESDAY

21—WEDNESDAY

22—THURSDAY

23—FRIDAY

24—SATURDAY

*"Martha, Martha, you are anxious and troubled
about many things, but one thing is necessary.
Mary has chosen the good portion, which
will not be taken away from her."*

LUKE 10:41-42 ESV

OCTOBER 2020

God wants us walking with Jesus. The more
we walk in His truth, the more light there
will be for the path before us and the less
stress and trip-ups we'll encounter.

25—SUNDAY

26—MONDAY

27—TUESDAY

28—WEDNESDAY

....

....

....

....

29—THURSDAY

....

....

....

....

30—FRIDAY

....

....

....

....

31—SATURDAY   *Halloween*

....

....

....

....

*If we claim that we experience a shared life
with him and continue to stumble around in
the dark, we're obviously lying through our
teeth—we're not living what we claim.*

1 JOHN 1:6 MSG

NOVEMBER 2020

SUNDAY	MONDAY	TUESDAY	WEDNESDAY
1 *Daylight Saving Time Ends*	2	3 *Election Day*	4
8	9	10	11 *Veterans Day*
15	16	17	18
22	23	24	25
29	30	1	2

THURSDAY	FRIDAY	SATURDAY
5	6	7
12	13	14
19	20	21
26	27	28
Thanksgiving Day		
3	4	5

Heart to Heart

God wants you to seek His face, for He knows that when you do, your heart, mind, and spirit will have their true focus. You will find His peace, His strength, His way. You will be more in line with His will for you because you have looked to Him before you even set your foot out the door or stuck your toe in the water.

Your spirit needs God's presence just as your body needs air, food, and water. God is aching to hear your voice. He's ready for that heart-to-heart talk that will energize you for the day. Seek. Speak. Listen. Then walk.

. . . .

Here I am, Lord, coming before You, seeking Your presence, breathing in Your Spirit, drinking in Your light, feeding on Your wisdom. Show me Your way.

GOALS *for this* MONTH

- [ ] ....
- [ ] ....
- [ ] ....
- [ ] ....
- [ ] ....
- [ ] ....
- [ ] ....
- [ ] ....
- [ ] ....
- [ ] ....
- [ ] ....
- [ ] ....

You have said, Seek My face [inquire for and require My presence as your vital need]. My heart says to You, Your face (Your presence), Lord, will I seek, inquire for, and require [of necessity and on the authority of Your Word].

PSALM 27:8 AMPC

NOVEMBER 2020

God is your stronghold. He is always there
waiting to help, to strengthen, to shower
you with love, peace, joy, and confidence,
to empower you to do all He's calling you to do.

1—SUNDAY *Daylight Saving Time Ends*

2—MONDAY

3—TUESDAY *Election Day*

4—WEDNESDAY

5—THURSDAY

6—FRIDAY

7—SATURDAY

*The Lord is the Refuge and Stronghold of
my life. . . . Though a host encamp against
me, my heart shall not fear; though war arise
against me, [even then] in this will I be confident.*

PSALM 27:1, 3 AMPC

NOVEMBER 2020

Rest easy and assured.
God's angels are watching over you.

8—SUNDAY

9—MONDAY

10—TUESDAY

11—WEDNESDAY

Veterans Day

....
....
....
....

12—THURSDAY

....
....
....
....

13—FRIDAY

....
....
....
....

14—SATURDAY

....
....
....
....

*He will give His angels [especial] charge over
you to accompany and defend and preserve
you in all your ways [of obedience and service].
They shall bear you up on their hands.*

PSALM 91:11–12 AMPC

NOVEMBER 2020

When was the last time you thanked God? What did you thank Him for? How can you make counting your blessings part of your regular routine?

15—SUNDAY

16—MONDAY

17—TUESDAY

18—WEDNESDAY

19—THURSDAY

20—FRIDAY

21—SATURDAY

"Oh, how my soul praises the Lord. How my spirit rejoices in God my Savior! For he took notice of his lowly servant girl.... For the Mighty One is holy, and he has done great things for me.... His mighty arm has done tremendous things!"

LUKE 1:46-49, 51 NLT

NOVEMBER 2020

God's going to make you victorious. Your role?
To remind yourself that He is in control and to
trust Him to whom the solution is a simple thing.

22—SUNDAY

23—MONDAY

24—TUESDAY

25—WEDNESDAY

....
....
....
....

26—THURSDAY   *Thanksgiving Day*

....
....
....
....

27—FRIDAY

....
....
....
....

28—SATURDAY

....
....
....
....

"You will see neither wind nor rain. . .but this valley
will be filled with water. You will have plenty. . . .
But this is only a simple thing for the LORD,
for he will make you victorious."

2 KINGS 3:17-18 NLT

DECEMBER 2020

SUNDAY	MONDAY	TUESDAY	WEDNESDAY
29	30	1	2
6	7	8	9
13	14	15	16
20	21 *First Day of Winter*	22	23
27	28	29	30

THURSDAY	FRIDAY	SATURDAY
3	4	5
10	11	12
Hanukkah Begins at Sundown		
17	18	19
24	25	26
Christmas Eve	*Christmas Day*	
31	1	2
New Year's Eve		

NOVEMBER

S	M	T	W	T	F	S
1	2	3	4	5	6	7
8	9	10	11	12	13	14
15	16	17	18	19	20	21
22	23	24	25	26	27	28
29	30					

JANUARY

S	M	T	W	T	F	S
					1	2
3	4	5	6	7	8	9
10	11	12	13	14	15	16
17	18	19	20	21	22	23
24	25	26	27	28	29	30
31						

Hanging On Tight

Nothing this week, month, year has worked out right. No matter how hard you try, nothing seems to be going your way. You are not only stressed out but feeling helpless, as if you're falling and no one is waiting to catch you.

Tell God how you're feeling, how much pressure you're under, how alone and hopeless you feel. As soon as you do, He'll grab hold of you and hang on tight. He'll calm you down, open your eyes to the blessings around you, and put a smile back on your face.

What are you waiting for? Take advantage of the One who has chosen you and vowed to walk with you, to talk to you like a friend. The One who will never, ever let you go.

. . . .

Jesus, I feel as if I'm slipping, falling.
Grab on to me. Never let me go.

GOALS *for this* MONTH

- [ ] ....
- [ ] ....
- [ ] ....
- [ ] ....
- [ ] ....
- [ ] ....
- [ ] ....
- [ ] ....
- [ ] ....
- [ ] ....
- [ ] ....
- [ ] ....

The minute I said, "I'm slipping, I'm falling,"
your love, GOD, took hold and held me fast.
When I was upset and beside myself,
you calmed me down and cheered me up.

PSALM 94:18–19 MSG

NOVEMBER–DECEMBER 2020

You know God has a purpose for your life.
Be assured that as long as you put everything
you're doing in His hands—leaving the results to
Him and Him alone—not only will your stress
abate, but God will make your plans succeed.

29—SUNDAY

30—MONDAY

1—TUESDAY

2—WEDNESDAY

3—THURSDAY

4—FRIDAY

5—SATURDAY

*Commit your actions to the LORD,
and your plans will succeed.*
PROVERBS 16:3 NLT

DECEMBER 2020

Let your stress melt away as you spend some time in God's presence today with the knowledge there is nothing you must do to prove yourself to Him.

6—SUNDAY

7—MONDAY

8—TUESDAY

9—WEDNESDAY

10—THURSDAY
Hanukkah Begins at Sundown

11—FRIDAY

12—SATURDAY

*"Don't be afraid; you are more valuable to
God than a whole flock of sparrows."*

MATTHEW 10:31 NLT

DECEMBER 2020

One way to keep yourself happy, healthy, and stress-free is to connect with like-minded people. And what better way to do that than through church! Gather for worship with fellow believers. Find or found a ministry that feeds a passion in your own life.

13—SUNDAY

14—MONDAY

15—TUESDAY

16—WEDNESDAY

17—THURSDAY

18—FRIDAY

19—SATURDAY

*Let's see how inventive we can be in encouraging
love and helping out, not avoiding worshiping
together as some do but spurring each other on.*

HEBREWS 10:24-25 MSG

DECEMBER 2020

Allow God's gift of laughter to heal you,
to lift you out of your stress and into His holy joy.

20–SUNDAY

21–MONDAY   *First Day of Winter*

22–TUESDAY

23—WEDNESDAY

24—THURSDAY

Christmas Eve

25—FRIDAY

Christmas Day

26—SATURDAY

*A cheerful disposition is good for your health;
gloom and doom leave you bone-tired.*

PROVERBS 17:22 MSG

DECEMBER 2020-JANUARY 2021

Dance before the Lord. Praise Him with
music and song. Pick up an instrument
and play for Him. Before you know it,
you'll be bringing joy to God and yourself!

27—SUNDAY

28—MONDAY

29—TUESDAY

30—WEDNESDAY

31—THURSDAY

New Year's Eve

1—FRIDAY

New Year's Day

2—SATURDAY

*David was dancing before the LORD with
great enthusiasm. . . . So David and all the
house of Israel were bringing the ark of the
LORD up [to the City of David] with shouts
[of joy] and with the sound of the trumpet.*

2 SAMUEL 6:14-15 AMP

JANUARY 2021

SUNDAY	MONDAY	TUESDAY	WEDNESDAY
27	28	29	30
3	4	5	6
10	11	12	13
17	18 *Martin Luther King Jr. Day*	19	20
24	25	26	27
31			

THURSDAY	FRIDAY	SATURDAY
31	1 *New Year's Day*	2
7	8	9
14	15	16
21	22	23
28	29	30

DECEMBER

S	M	T	W	T	F	S
		1	2	3	4	5
6	7	8	9	10	11	12
13	14	15	16	17	18	19
20	21	22	23	24	25	26
27	28	29	30	31		

FEBRUARY

S	M	T	W	T	F	S
	1	2	3	4	5	6
7	8	9	10	11	12	13
14	15	16	17	18	19	20
21	22	23	24	25	26	27
28						

Are You There?

During Jesus' time on earth, no matter what was happening in His life, no matter how many people were vying for His attention, He kept His eyes on His Father. He went alone to a quiet place where He could get calm, focus, and spend time in the company of the Master Creator. This time of solitude and single-minded devotion allowed Him to come away refreshed, rejuvenated, replenished, ready to give His entire attention to those who came to Him.

Are you there for Jesus? Are you there for God? Are you there for others? Are you even there for yourself?

Unplug yourself from the world—including your phone, computer, TV, and radio—a few times a week, at least. Plug into God, Jesus, the Spirit. Spend time with the Creator and His creation. Then use that energy and power to plug into yourself and those around you. Focus, be fed, then feed. Be there.

. . . .

Lord, help me to be there for You, myself, and others. Be the reigning power in my life once again!

GOALS *for this* MONTH

- [ ] ....
- [ ] ....
- [ ] ....
- [ ] ....
- [ ] ....
- [ ] ....
- [ ] ....
- [ ] ....
- [ ] ....
- [ ] ....
- [ ] ....
- [ ] ....

Let us also lay aside every weight...
looking to Jesus, the founder
and perfecter of our faith.
HEBREWS 12:1-2 ESV

JANUARY 2021

Look for the best in others. And see
what happens within your own self.

3—SUNDAY

4—MONDAY

5—TUESDAY

6—WEDNESDAY

7—THURSDAY

8—FRIDAY

9—SATURDAY

"I'm telling you to love your enemies. Let them bring out the best in you, not the worst. When someone gives you a hard time, respond with the energies of prayer, for then you are working out of your true selves, your God-created selves."

MATTHEW 5:44–45 MSG

JANUARY 2021

You can always meet God in the quiet place of your heart. Allow your spirit to go deep, to call to and be answered by the Holy Spirit within. Know His song is with you.

10—SUNDAY

11—MONDAY

12—TUESDAY

13—WEDNESDAY

14—THURSDAY

15—FRIDAY

16—SATURDAY

Why are you in despair, O my soul? And why have you become restless and disturbed within me? Hope in God and wait expectantly for Him, for I shall again praise Him for the help of His presence.

PSALM 42:5 AMP

JANUARY 2021

Spend time with God, an open Bible upon your lap.
Rest assured that God will give you the wisdom
to make the right decision in His eyes.

17—SUNDAY

18—MONDAY   *Martin Luther King Jr. Day*

19—TUESDAY

20—WEDNESDAY

21—THURSDAY

22—FRIDAY

23—SATURDAY

*Such things were written in the Scriptures
long ago to teach us. And the Scriptures
give us hope and encouragement as we wait
patiently for God's promises to be fulfilled.*

ROMANS 15:4 NLT

JANUARY 2021

Sometimes we get so caught up in our lives,
so stressed out, that we don't recognize where
God may be directing our attention, the solutions
He might be providing if only we'd look or
listen, whether through circumstances, prayer,
the wisdom of others, or the scriptures.

24—SUNDAY

25—MONDAY

26—TUESDAY

27—WEDNESDAY

28—THURSDAY

29—FRIDAY

30—SATURDAY

*Simon answered, "Master, we toiled all night and took
nothing! But at your word I will let down the nets."
And when they had done this, they enclosed a large
number of fish, and their nets were breaking.*

LUKE 5:5-6 ESV

FEBRUARY 2021

SUNDAY	MONDAY	TUESDAY	WEDNESDAY
31	1	2	3
7	8	9	10
14 *Valentine's Day*	15 *Presidents' Day*	16	17 *Ash Wednesday*
21	22	23	24
28	1	2	3

THURSDAY	FRIDAY	SATURDAY
4	5	6
11	12	13
18	19	20
25	26	27
4	5	6

JANUARY

S	M	T	W	T	F	S
					1	2
3	4	5	6	7	8	9
10	11	12	13	14	15	16
17	18	19	20	21	22	23
24	25	26	27	28	29	30
31						

MARCH

S	M	T	W	T	F	S
	1	2	3	4	5	6
7	8	9	10	11	12	13
14	15	16	17	18	19	20
21	22	23	24	25	26	27
28	29	30	31			

Patiently Ponder in Prayer

Events you never foresaw are happening all around you. There is so much going on, so much commotion in your world and life that your thoughts are pitter-pattering like so many raindrops splashing onto a tin roof. You begin losing sleep in the night hours, wondering what will happen next or how you can keep what you *think* is going to happen from happening. In the daytime, your judgment becomes skewed. You have so many thoughts careening around in your head, you can no longer take information in.

What's missing in your life? Patiently pondering in prayer, trusting that God is with you and will reveal things in His own good time. As Mother Teresa said, "Prayer is not asking. Prayer is putting oneself in the hands of God, at His disposition, and listening to His voice in the depths of our hearts."

. . . .

Lord, help me to pray, ponder, and put myself
in Your hands as You speak to my heart.

GOALS *for this* MONTH

- [ ] ....
- [ ] ....
- [ ] ....
- [ ] ....
- [ ] ....
- [ ] ....
- [ ] ....
- [ ] ....
- [ ] ....
- [ ] ....
- [ ] ....
- [ ] ....

*Mary was keeping within herself
all these things (sayings), weighing
and pondering them in her heart.*

LUKE 2:19 AMPC

JANUARY-FEBRUARY 2021

Have a decision to make? A path to choose? Looking for direction? For peace? God has all the answers for you and even outlines them in Jeremiah 6:16.

31—SUNDAY

1—MONDAY

2—TUESDAY

3—WEDNESDAY

4—THURSDAY

5—FRIDAY

6—SATURDAY

Stand by the roads and look; and ask for the eternal paths, where the good, old way is; then walk in it, and you will find rest for your souls. But they said, We will not walk in it!

JEREMIAH 6:16 AMPC

FEBRUARY 2021

God sees so much more than you do.
Your role is to seek His knowledge,
let Him have His say, then do as He wills,
regardless of how much sense it makes to you.

7—SUNDAY

8—MONDAY

9—TUESDAY

10—WEDNESDAY

11—THURSDAY

12—FRIDAY

13—SATURDAY

*The LORD said to Samuel, "Don't judge by
his appearance or height, for I have rejected
him. The LORD doesn't see things the way you
see them. People judge by outward appearance,
but the LORD looks at the heart."*

1 SAMUEL 16:7 NLT

FEBRUARY 2021

God wants you to be a *God* follower more than just a *rule* follower. All you have to do is listen and obey. Make His will yours.

14—SUNDAY   *Valentine's Day*

15—MONDAY   *Presidents' Day*

16—TUESDAY

17—WEDNESDAY   *Ash Wednesday*

....
....
....
....

18—THURSDAY

....
....
....
....

19—FRIDAY

....
....
....
....

20—SATURDAY

....
....
....
....

*"God removed Saul and replaced him with David,
a man about whom God said, 'I have found
David son of Jesse, a man after my own heart.
He will do everything I want him to do.'"*

ACTS 13:22 NLT

FEBRUARY 2021

Allow prayer to be your creative and limitless endeavor. Go to God. Seek Him with your whole heart, and He will expand your world.

21–SUNDAY

22–MONDAY

23–TUESDAY

24—WEDNESDAY

25—THURSDAY

26—FRIDAY

27—SATURDAY

Then you will seek Me, inquire for, and require Me [as a vital necessity] and find Me when you search for Me with all your heart.

JEREMIAH 29:13 AMPC

MARCH 2021

SUNDAY	MONDAY	TUESDAY	WEDNESDAY
28	1	2	3
7	8	9	10
14 *Daylight Saving Time Begins*	15	16	17 *St. Patrick's Day*
21	22	23	24
28 *Palm Sunday*	29	30	31

THURSDAY	FRIDAY	SATURDAY
4	5	6
11	12	13
18	19	20 *First Day of Spring*
25	26	27 *Passover Begins at Sundown*
1	2	3

Lessons to Learn

Ralph Waldo Emerson said, "No man ever prayed heartily without learning something."

What is your prayer life like? Do you take the things that are stressing you out and present them to God? Do you put your entire heart into the endeavor? Do you ask God to show you what He wants you to see before you open up His Word? Are you persistently asking, seeking, and knocking on His door (see Matthew 7:7)? Are you allowing yourself to be vulnerable, letting Him into your world—heart, mind, body, spirit, and soul—opening the door where He is seeking entry (see Revelation 3:20)?

God has good things in store for you, wisdom to impart, words to heal, love to give, lessons to learn. Look. Listen. Learn.

. . . .

Lord, I come before You, seeking You with my entire being. Teach me what You would have me know. In Jesus' name. Amen.

GOALS *for this* MONTH

- [ ] ....
- [ ] ....
- [ ] ....
- [ ] ....
- [ ] ....
- [ ] ....
- [ ] ....
- [ ] ....
- [ ] ....
- [ ] ....
- [ ] ....

"As it is written in the Scriptures, 'They will all be taught by God.' Everyone who listens to the Father and learns from him comes to me."

JOHN 6:45 NLT

FEBRUARY-MARCH 2021

When was the last time you took time out with God, returned to Him, rested in Him, and came away quieter within and, having heard Him speak, more confident in Him? Try a time-out with God today. The length is up to you—and Him.

28—SUNDAY

1—MONDAY

2—TUESDAY

3—WEDNESDAY

4—THURSDAY

5—FRIDAY

6—SATURDAY

The Sovereign LORD. . .says: "Only in returning to me and resting in me will you be saved. In quietness and confidence is your strength." . . . Your own ears will hear him. Right behind you a voice will say, "This is the way you should go," whether to the right or to the left.

ISAIAH 30:15, 21 NLT

MARCH 2021

See yourself as an eternal creature
who has been given God's breath of life,
who has been endowed with a soul, and
you'll find yourself more awed than anxious.

7—SUNDAY

8—MONDAY

9—TUESDAY

10—WEDNESDAY

....
....
....
....

11—THURSDAY

....
....
....
....

12—FRIDAY

....
....
....
....

13—SATURDAY

....
....
....
....

So those who received his word were baptized, and there were added that day about three thousand souls. And they devoted themselves to the apostles' teaching and the fellowship, to the breaking of bread and the prayers. And awe came upon every soul.

ACTS 2:41-43 ESV

MARCH 2021

God says, "Be still, and know that I am God"
(Psalm 46:10 ESV). *You* are not. But *He* is.
And He is with you—always and in all ways.

14—SUNDAY   *Daylight Saving Time Begins*

15—MONDAY

16—TUESDAY

17—WEDNESDAY   *St. Patrick's Day*

....

....

....

....

18—THURSDAY

....

....

....

....

19—FRIDAY

....

....

....

....

20—SATURDAY   *First Day of Spring*

....

....

....

....

*God is our refuge and strength, a very
present help in trouble. Therefore we will not
fear though the earth gives way, though the
mountains be moved into the heart of the sea.*

PSALM 46:1-2 ESV

MARCH 2021

Be still. Relax in your heavenly Father's arms. Lean back. Breathe deep. Feel His heartbeat. You are home. Let Him carry you.

21—SUNDAY

22—MONDAY

23—TUESDAY

24—WEDNESDAY

25—THURSDAY

26—FRIDAY

27—SATURDAY   *Passover Begins at Sundown*

He will feed his flock like a shepherd.
He will carry the lambs in his arms,
holding them close to his heart.
ISAIAH 40:11 NLT

MARCH-APRIL 2021

No matter what has happened, is happening,
or might happen, God is with you. He is
personally at your side. He will give you
rest. "Everything will be fine for you."

28—SUNDAY

Palm Sunday

29—MONDAY

30—TUESDAY

31—WEDNESDAY

1—THURSDAY

2—FRIDAY   *Good Friday*

3—SATURDAY

*The Lord replied, "I will personally go
with you...and I will give you rest—
everything will be fine for you."*
EXODUS 33:14 NLT

APRIL 2021

SUNDAY	MONDAY	TUESDAY	WEDNESDAY
28	29	30	31
4	5	6	7
Easter			
11	12	13	14
18	19	20	21
25	26	27	28

THURSDAY	FRIDAY	SATURDAY
1	2	3
	Good Friday	
8	9	10
15	16	17
22	23	24
29	30	1
	Arbor Day	

MARCH

S	M	T	W	T	F	S
		1	2	3	4	5	6
7	8	9	10	11	12	13
14	15	16	17	18	19	20
21	22	23	24	25	26	27
28	29	30	31			

MAY

S	M	T	W	T	F	S
						1
2	3	4	5	6	7	8
9	10	11	12	13	14	15
16	17	18	19	20	21	22
23	24	25	26	27	28	29
30	31					

See the Trees

God wants you out and about, looking at His creation, learning its lessons, breathing in its beauty, praising its presence, allowing it to speak. Amazingly enough, looking at trees—the more the better—will relieve your stress! Both exercising amid the boughs and just looking at them will lower your blood pressure and lift your mood. What an amazing God you have, who has given you a simple way to lower your stress.

Whether you live in the city or the country, find a tree or three or more. Beat a path to a forest floor. Or simply stare at some trees from your window. Take a few deep belly breaths. Praise God for the trees' beauty and power to lift your spirits. See the trees and ease the stress.

. . . .

Thank You, Lord, for the tranquility of Your trees.

GOALS *for this* MONTH

- ☐ ....
- ☐ ....
- ☐ ....
- ☐ ....
- ☐ ....
- ☐ ....
- ☐ ....
- ☐ ....
- ☐ ....
- ☐ ....
- ☐ ....
- ☐ ....

*"Ask the birds of the air, and let them tell you;
or speak to the earth [with its many forms of
life], and it will teach you; and let the fish
of the sea declare [this truth] to you."*

JOB 12:7-8 AMP

APRIL 2021

Feel God's presence. Recognize He is above, below, within, and without. With these ideas at the forefront of your mind and the awareness of His love in the depths of your soul, there is no room for fight, flight, or freeze. Simply peace as you live, move, and have your being.

4—SUNDAY *Easter*

5—MONDAY

6—TUESDAY

7—WEDNESDAY

8—THURSDAY

9—FRIDAY

10—SATURDAY

*They should seek God, in the hope that they
might feel after Him and find Him, although
He is not far from each one of us. For in Him
we live and move and have our being.*

ACTS 17:27-28 AMPC

APRIL 2021

Prayer is a force that can shake open doors,
make chains fall away, and set prisoners free.
With all this power, prayer obviously can release
your stress, make your burdens fall away,
and change your limited perspective. All you
need to do is believe it is possible.

11—SUNDAY

12—MONDAY

13—TUESDAY

14—WEDNESDAY

15—THURSDAY

16—FRIDAY

17—SATURDAY

*Paul and Silas were praying and singing
hymns to God.... Suddenly, there was a massive
earthquake, and the prison was shaken to its
foundations. All the doors immediately flew open,
and the chains of every prisoner fell off!*

ACTS 16:25-26 NLT

APRIL 2021

Let God know what's going on in your life.
He will listen. He will see. He will reach down
and lift you up to safety, give you the security
you crave, and help you steer clear of snags.

18—SUNDAY

19—MONDAY

20—TUESDAY

21—WEDNESDAY

22—THURSDAY

23—FRIDAY

24—SATURDAY

He drew me up out of a horrible pit [a pit of tumult and of destruction], out of the miry clay (froth and slime), and set my feet upon a rock, steadying my steps and establishing my goings.

PSALM 40:2 AMPC

God hears your prayers, whether said aloud or silently. And when you look to Him for help, baring your heart to Him, He will meet you more than halfway. He'll free you from stress and fear. He'll rescue you.

25—SUNDAY

26—MONDAY

27—TUESDAY

28—WEDNESDAY

29—THURSDAY

30—FRIDAY   *Arbor Day*

1—SATURDAY

*GOD met me more than halfway, he freed me
from my anxious fears. Look at him; give him
your warmest smile. Never hide your feelings
from him. When I was desperate, I called out,
and GOD got me out of a tight spot.*

PSALM 34:4–6 MSG

MAY 2021

SUNDAY	MONDAY	TUESDAY	WEDNESDAY
25	26	27	28
2	3	4	5
9	10	11	12
Mother's Day			
16	17	18	19
23	24	25	26
30	31 *Memorial Day*		

THURSDAY	FRIDAY	SATURDAY
29	30	1
6	7	8
National Day of Prayer		
13	14	15
20	21	22
27	28	29

Circle of Protection

Amid a stressful situation in which you see no way out—mentally, physically, emotionally, spiritually—go to God. As soon as you're in His presence, He'll set up, between you and whatever's coming against you, a protective barrier. See it. Know it's there. Do not doubt. Then open your mouth and pray. Realize how good God is. Praise Him for what He's doing in your life. Know that even if you still don't see a way out, that's okay. You're with the Master Planner and Protector. He's got you covered. He has an exit plan. He has good things lined up and coming your way. Then rest in His peace.

I see no way out of this, Lord, but I know You do.
And in You I trust. In You I have peace.

GOALS *for this* MONTH

- ☐ ....
- ☐ ....
- ☐ ....
- ☐ ....
- ☐ ....
- ☐ ....
- ☐ ....
- ☐ ....
- ☐ ....
- ☐ ....
- ☐ ....
- ☐ ....

GOD's angel sets up a circle of protection around us while we pray. Open your mouth and taste, open your eyes and see—how good GOD is. Blessed are you who run to him. Worship GOD if you want the best; worship opens doors to all his goodness.

PSALM 34:7-9 MSG

MAY 2021

God is listening and ready to rescue you,
to help you catch your breath. He'll do it
every time. His job is to be there for you.
Your job is to reach out for Him.

2—SUNDAY

3—MONDAY

4—TUESDAY

5—WEDNESDAY

6—THURSDAY   *National Day of Prayer*

7—FRIDAY

8—SATURDAY

Is anyone crying for help? GOD is listening, ready to rescue you. If your heart is broken, you'll find GOD right there; if you're kicked in the gut, he'll help you catch your breath. Disciples so often get into trouble; still, GOD is there every time.

PSALM 34:17–19 MSG

MAY 2021

Call. And God will respond and
give you all the strength you need.
Then thank Him with your whole heart.

9—SUNDAY *Mother's Day*

10—MONDAY

11—TUESDAY

12—WEDNESDAY

13—THURSDAY

14—FRIDAY

15—SATURDAY

I give you thanks, O Lord, with my whole heart. . . .
On the day I called, you answered me;
my strength of soul you increased.

PSALM 138:1, 3 ESV

MAY 2021

Take heart. God is working out all plans in
your favor. Just continue hoping, trusting,
praying. Your Deliverer is right next to you,
standing by you, keeping you safe and sound!

16—SUNDAY

17—MONDAY

18—TUESDAY

19—WEDNESDAY

20—THURSDAY

21—FRIDAY

22—SATURDAY

*No one stood by me. They all ran like scared
rabbits. But it doesn't matter—the Master stood
by me and helped me. . . . God's looking after me,
keeping me safe in the kingdom of heaven.*

2 TIMOTHY 4:16-18 MSG

MAY 2021

Put no limits on God. Simply look
to Jesus and expect beyond the best!

23—SUNDAY

24—MONDAY

25—TUESDAY

26—WEDNESDAY

27—THURSDAY

28—FRIDAY

29—SATURDAY

Seeing Peter and John about to go into the temple, he asked to receive alms. And Peter directed his gaze at him, as did John, and said, "Look at us." And he fixed his attention on them, expecting to receive something from them.

ACTS 3:3-5 ESV

JUNE 2021

SUNDAY	MONDAY	TUESDAY	WEDNESDAY
30	31	1	2
6	7	8	9
13	14 *Flag Day*	15	16
20 *Father's Day*	21 *First Day of Summer*	22	23
27	28	29	30

THURSDAY	FRIDAY	SATURDAY
3	4	5
10	11	12
17	18	19
24	25	26
1	2	3

Aiming to Please and Praise

Sometimes women get stressed out looking for love, recognition, contentment, and satisfaction in all the wrong places. Leah, knowing her husband, Jacob, had been tricked into marrying her, did all she could to win at least a portion of Jacob's love away from her barren sister Rachel. Leah named her firstborn Reuben (*See, it's a boy!*), thinking that effort would make Jacob love her. The second she named Simeon, as she realized *God* had *heard* her prayers. The third she named Levi, *companion*, thinking now Jacob would connect with her. Finally, she had Judah, saying, "Now I'll *praise God*."

Amid our prayerful expectations, we would be wise to acknowledge, thank, and praise God for the comfort He continually gives us, even when our prayers are not answered exactly as we'd hoped, for the Lord alone should be the One we aim to please and praise in our lives.

. . . .

*I praise You, Lord, for all You have
done and are doing in my life!*

GOALS *for this* MONTH

- ☐ ....
- ☐ ....
- ☐ ....
- ☐ ....
- ☐ ....
- ☐ ....
- ☐ ....
- ☐ ....
- ☐ ....
- ☐ ....
- ☐ ....
- ☐ ....

She said, "This time I'll praise GOD."
So she named him Judah (Praise-GOD).

GENESIS 29:35 MSG

MAY-JUNE 2021

Move out of your stress and into
God's strength—and dance!

30—SUNDAY

31—MONDAY

Memorial Day

1—TUESDAY

2—WEDNESDAY

3—THURSDAY

4—FRIDAY

5—SATURDAY

This is my prayer. That God...will give you spiritual wisdom and the insight to know more of him: that you may receive that inner illumination of the spirit which will make you realise how great is the hope to which he is calling you...and how tremendous is the power available to us who believe in God.

EPHESIANS 1:17-19 PHILLIPS

JUNE 2021

God constantly tells us of the plenty
surrounding us. He knows exactly
what we need and will provide it.

6—SUNDAY

7—MONDAY

8—TUESDAY

9—WEDNESDAY

10—THURSDAY

11—FRIDAY

12—SATURDAY

*Every beast of the forest is Mine,
and the cattle upon a thousand hills or
upon the mountains where thousands are.*

PSALM 50:10 AMPC

JUNE 2021

When we put God's truth up against the false worries that tend to drown us out, we find ourselves back with our Shepherd, beside the still waters.

13—SUNDAY

14—MONDAY

Flag Day

15—TUESDAY

16—WEDNESDAY

17—THURSDAY

18—FRIDAY

19—SATURDAY

God did not give us a spirit of timidity (of cowardice, of craven and cringing and fawning fear), but [He has given us a spirit] of power and of love and of calm and well-balanced mind and discipline and self-control.

2 TIMOTHY 1:7 AMPC

JUNE 2021

Go to God in prayer and ask where your priorities might differ from His. Then begin revising your stride to keep pace with His rhythm on His good path.

20—SUNDAY   *Father's Day*

....

....

....

....

21—MONDAY   *First Day of Summer*

....

....

....

....

22—TUESDAY

....

....

....

....

23—WEDNESDAY

24—THURSDAY

25—FRIDAY

26—SATURDAY

"May GOD, our very own God. . .keep us centered and devoted to him, following the life path he has cleared, watching the signposts, walking at the pace and rhythms he laid down for our ancestors."

1 KINGS 8:57-58 MSG

JUNE–JULY 2021

Immerse yourself in God's Word, pray,
welcome His Spirit, expect the Lord is
acting on your behalf, and leave the results
to Him. His part is to work wonders.

27—SUNDAY

28—MONDAY

29—TUESDAY

30—WEDNESDAY

....
....
....
....

1—THURSDAY

....
....
....
....

2—FRIDAY

....
....
....
....

3—SATURDAY

....
....
....

*"Now, Lord. . .grant to your servants to continue
to speak your word with all boldness, while you
stretch out your hand to heal, and signs and
wonders are performed through the name of your
holy servant Jesus." And when they had prayed. . .
they were all filled with the Holy Spirit and
continued to speak the word of God with boldness.*

ACTS 4:29–31 ESV

JULY 2021

SUNDAY	MONDAY	TUESDAY	WEDNESDAY
27	28	29	30
4 *Independence Day*	5	6	7
11	12	13	14
18	19	20	21
25	26	27	28

THURSDAY	FRIDAY	SATURDAY
1	2	3
8	9	10
15	16	17
22	23	24
29	30	31

JUNE

S	M	T	W	T	F	S
			1	2	3	4	5
6	7	8	9	10	11	12
13	14	15	16	17	18	19
20	21	22	23	24	25	26
27	28	29	30			

AUGUST

S	M	T	W	T	F	S
1	2	3	4	5	6	7
8	9	10	11	12	13	14
15	16	17	18	19	20	21
22	23	24	25	26	27	28
29	30	31				

Recognition

Sometimes the symptoms of stress can be quite obvious—low energy, nervousness, loss of focus, sleeplessness, weakness, timidity, jumpiness, tenseness, etc.—all of which keep others (and ourselves, perhaps) from recognizing that we have been with Jesus. For His persona exudes the exact opposite characteristics. Jesus is tireless, calm, focused, rested, bold, peaceful, and relaxed.

Spend time each day with Jesus. When you do, His characteristics will rub off on you bit by bit. Each day you will become more like Him until one day, people will look at you and recognize you have spent time in the presence of Jesus.

. . . .

At this point, Jesus, I'm not sure what—
or who—people see when they look at me.
So I'm coming to spend time with You,
imbibing Your peace, strength, boldness,
and so much more. May I grow each day to look
more like You than anything or anyone else.

GOALS *for this* MONTH

- [ ] ....
- [ ] ....
- [ ] ....
- [ ] ....
- [ ] ....
- [ ] ....
- [ ] ....
- [ ] ....
- [ ] ....
- [ ] ....
- [ ] ....
- [ ] ....

Now when they saw the boldness of Peter and John, and perceived that they were uneducated, common men, they were astonished. And they recognized that they had been with Jesus.

ACTS 4:13 ESV

JULY 2021

See every event and seeming setback as neither good nor bad but rather as a chance to pray and see the opportunity God is presenting you.

4—SUNDAY   *Independence Day*

....

....

....

....

5—MONDAY

....

....

....

....

6—TUESDAY

....

....

....

....

7—WEDNESDAY

....

....

....

....

8—THURSDAY

....

....

....

....

9—FRIDAY

....

....

....

....

10—SATURDAY

....

....

....

....

*Now ask and keep on asking and you
will receive, so that your joy (gladness,
delight) may be full and complete.*
JOHN 16:24 AMPC

JULY 2021

Consider your priorities today. Have you
made time for God, secure in the knowledge
that everything else will fall into place
once He's number one in your life?

11—SUNDAY

12—MONDAY

13—TUESDAY

14—WEDNESDAY

15—THURSDAY

16—FRIDAY

17—SATURDAY

"So don't worry and don't keep saying, 'What shall we eat...drink or...wear?'... Set your heart on the kingdom and his goodness, and all these things will come to you as a matter of course."

MATTHEW 6:31, 33 PHILLIPS

JULY 2021

Throw off the angst and put on Christ's peace.
Let go of sorrow and reach out for His joy. Look
away from your lack and focus on His abundance.

18—SUNDAY

19—MONDAY

20—TUESDAY

21–WEDNESDAY

22–THURSDAY

23–FRIDAY

24–SATURDAY

*Throw off your old sinful nature and your former
way of life, which is corrupted by lust and deception.
Instead, let the Spirit renew your thoughts and
attitudes. Put on your new nature, created to
be like God—truly righteous and holy.*

EPHESIANS 4:22-24 NLT

JULY 2021

Make it a daily endeavor to delve into God's
Word. If you have a good half hour, soak in
His wisdom. If you have less than that,
even only one minute, ask God to show
you what He would have you know today.

25—SUNDAY

26—MONDAY

27—TUESDAY

28—WEDNESDAY

29—THURSDAY

30—FRIDAY

31—SATURDAY

My child, pay attention to what I say. Listen carefully to my words. Don't lose sight of them. Let them penetrate deep into your heart, for they bring life to those who find them, and healing to their whole body.

PROVERBS 4:20-22 NLT

AUGUST 2021

SUNDAY	MONDAY	TUESDAY	WEDNESDAY
1	2	3	4
8	9	10	11
15	16	17	18
22	23	24	25
29	30	31	1

THURSDAY	FRIDAY	SATURDAY
5	6	7
12	13	14
19	20	21
26	27	28
2	3	4

Faithful Investment

Before going on a long trip, a nobleman divides ten pounds of silver between three servants, saying, "Invest this for me while I am gone" (Luke 19:13 NLT). When the nobleman returns as king, the first servant reports he invested his portion of the master's money and increased it tenfold. The second says his investment increased fivefold. Both of these servants are rewarded according to how they profited. But the last servant, who, fearing the master, did nothing but hide his master's money to keep it safe, is stripped of what he was given.

The point is that God wants you to invest the gifts He's given you but not stress over the results. Your responsibility is to do only what He asks. Then relax, leaving the results to Him, and return for further orders, rejoicing over a task completed in His name.

. . . .

Lord, show me how to invest the gifts You've given me then leave the results to You alone.

GOALS *for this* MONTH

- [ ] ....
- [ ] ....
- [ ] ....
- [ ] ....
- [ ] ....
- [ ] ....
- [ ] ....
- [ ] ....
- [ ] ....
- [ ] ....
- [ ] ....

" 'Well done!' the king exclaimed. 'You are a good servant. You have been faithful with the little I entrusted to you.' "

LUKE 19:17 NLT

AUGUST 2021

Stop for a moment. Ask yourself whose influence you are under during most of your day. Then consider how you can put yourself under *God's* influence 24-7 through prayer.

1—SUNDAY

2—MONDAY

3—TUESDAY

4—WEDNESDAY

5—THURSDAY

6—FRIDAY

7—SATURDAY

"Teacher," they said, "we know that you speak and teach what is right and are not influenced by what others think. You teach the way of God truthfully."

LUKE 20:21 NLT

AUGUST 2021

Don't stress. You have a quiet power.
Prayer is a part of that power.
Stress less, pray more.

8–SUNDAY

9–MONDAY

10–TUESDAY

11—WEDNESDAY

12—THURSDAY

13—FRIDAY

14—SATURDAY

*In quietness and in [trusting]
confidence shall be your strength.*
ISAIAH 30:15 AMPC

AUGUST 2021

God's not only your Comforter, Counselor,
Motivator, and Life Source. He's the One
who'll change your attitude (see Romans 12:2)
and your altitude, drawing you ever closer to
the God of your heart, mind, body, and soul.

15—SUNDAY

16—MONDAY

17—TUESDAY

18—WEDNESDAY

19—THURSDAY

20—FRIDAY

21—SATURDAY

Be careful how you live. . . . Make the most of every opportunity. . . . Don't act thoughtlessly, but understand what the Lord wants you to do. . . . Be filled with the Holy Spirit. . .making music to the Lord in your hearts.

EPHESIANS 5:15-19 NLT

AUGUST 2021

Know that God will help you do what
needs to be done each day, and the rest
will wait. Slow and steady will win the race.

22—SUNDAY

23—MONDAY

24—TUESDAY

25—WEDNESDAY

26—THURSDAY

27—FRIDAY

28—SATURDAY

The thoughts of the [steadily] diligent tend only to plenteousness, but everyone who is impatient and hasty hastens only to want.

PROVERBS 21:5 AMPC

SEPTEMBER 2021

SUNDAY	MONDAY	TUESDAY	WEDNESDAY
29	30	31	1
5	6	7	8
	Labor Day		
12	13	14	15
19	20	21	22
			First Day of Autumn/ See You at the Pole
26	27	28	29

THURSDAY	FRIDAY	SATURDAY
2	3	4
9	10	11
16	17	18
23	24	25
30	1	2

S	M	T	W	T	F	S
	1	2	3	4	5	6	7
8	9	10	11	12	13	14
15	16	17	18	19	20	21
22	23	24	25	26	27	28
29	30	31				

OCTOBER

S	M	T	W	T	F	S
					1	2
3	4	5	6	7	8	9
10	11	12	13	14	15	16
17	18	19	20	21	22	23
24	25	26	27	28	29	30
31						

Natural Rhythm

Take a moment right now to get away with Jesus. In His presence, you can find, get back, your true life— your life in and with Him. Only He can show you how to take a real break, one that includes His peace, His love, His strength, His nurturing. He is longing for you to take His hand, walk with Him, work with Him, play with Him. Jesus has set you an example, showing you how to spend more time with Father God. How to go up to the mountain alone and pray.

Learn the natural rhythm of God's good grace. He is waiting to show you. Are you willing to learn from Him and turn from the stress that dogs your steps?

. . . .

Lord, I'm willing to learn Your rhythm.
Help me recover my life!

GOALS *for this* MONTH

- [ ] ....
- [ ] ....
- [ ] ....
- [ ] ....
- [ ] ....
- [ ] ....
- [ ] ....
- [ ] ....
- [ ] ....
- [ ] ....
- [ ] ....
- [ ] ....

"Come to me. Get away with me and you'll recover your life. I'll show you how to take a real rest. Walk with me and work with me—watch how I do it. Learn the unforced rhythms of grace."

MATTHEW 11:28-30 MSG

AUGUST-SEPTEMBER 2021

God wants you to come to Him with everything—
no matter how trivial you might think it is. As you
pray, pepper your petitions with praises. Doing so
will not only change your perspective but also
give you a sense of God's peace.

29—SUNDAY

30—MONDAY

31—TUESDAY

1—WEDNESDAY

2—THURSDAY

3—FRIDAY

4—SATURDAY

Let petitions and praises shape your worries into prayers, letting God know your concerns. Before you know it, a sense of God's wholeness, everything coming together for good, will come and settle you down. It's wonderful what happens when Christ displaces worry at the center of your life.

PHILIPPIANS 4:6-7 MSG

SEPTEMBER 2021

Only in God's arms, His presence, His light are we truly safe, trusting that as He is with us in the dark night, He will yet be with us in the morning light.

5—SUNDAY

6—MONDAY *Labor Day*

7—TUESDAY

8—WEDNESDAY

9—THURSDAY

10—FRIDAY

11—SATURDAY

*In peace I will both lie down and sleep,
for You, Lord, alone make me dwell
in safety and confident trust.*
PSALM 4:8 AMPC

SEPTEMBER 2021

Make your thoughts more like God's
and you'll transform your world.

12—SUNDAY

13—MONDAY

14—TUESDAY

15—WEDNESDAY

16—THURSDAY

17—FRIDAY

18—SATURDAY

*"For my thoughts are not your thoughts,
neither are your ways my ways, declares the
LORD. For as the heavens are higher than the
earth, so are my ways higher than your ways
and my thoughts than your thoughts."*

ISAIAH 55:8-9 ESV

SEPTEMBER 2021

Put your wholehearted belief behind God's
promises. Claim that nothing is impossible.

19—SUNDAY

20—MONDAY

21—TUESDAY

22—WEDNESDAY   *First Day of Autumn/See You at the Pole*

23—THURSDAY

24—FRIDAY

25—SATURDAY

"Embrace this God-life. . .and nothing will be too much for you. This mountain, for instance: Just say, 'Go jump in the lake'—no shuffling or shilly-shallying— and it's as good as done. That's why I urge you to pray for absolutely everything."

MARK 11:22-24 MSG

SEPTEMBER-OCTOBER 2021

We need to delve daily into the Word, believe
God's promises, walk in His way, and pray, pray,
pray. When we do, we realize we don't need
to do it all. But for what He wants us to do,
He'll give us all the strength we need.

26—SUNDAY

27—MONDAY

28—TUESDAY

29—WEDNESDAY

30—THURSDAY

1—FRIDAY

2—SATURDAY

*I have strength for all things in Christ Who empowers
me [I am ready for anything and equal to anything
through Him Who infuses inner strength into me;
I am self-sufficient in Christ's sufficiency].*

PHILIPPIANS 4:13 AMPC

OCTOBER 2021

SUNDAY	MONDAY	TUESDAY	WEDNESDAY
26	27	28	29
3	4	5	6
10	11 *Columbus Day*	12	13
17	18	19	20
24	25	26	27
Halloween 31			

THURSDAY	FRIDAY	SATURDAY
30	1	2
7	8	9
14	15	16
21	22	23
28	29	30

A New Song

What song was in your head this morning? What might you have been mindlessly humming this afternoon? What might be "playing" in your head this evening? What chorus might you hear when your head hits the pillow?

Homing in on what we're humming and changing up the song can transform our lives. And when we change up that song in our heads to echo one of God's promises or truths, we are, in effect, worshipping our great God.

The most effective way of doing this is to claim each thought. What is it telling you? Does it agree with God's promises or truths? If not, replace it with what God would have you think. In effect, you'll be using God's amazing Word to overpower what the deceiver may have planted in your brain. Here's a general song to help you begin disarming the lies that lead to stress:

. . . .

"The Lord is my Shepherd [to feed, guide, and shield me], I shall not lack" (Psalm 23:1 AMPC).

GOALS *for this* MONTH

- [ ] ....
- [ ] ....
- [ ] ....
- [ ] ....
- [ ] ....
- [ ] ....
- [ ] ....
- [ ] ....
- [ ] ....
- [ ] ....
- [ ] ....
- [ ] ....

Sing GOD a brand-new song!
Earth and everyone in it, sing!
Sing to GOD—worship GOD!

PSALM 96:1–2 MSG

OCTOBER 2021

As you forgive others, God forgives you!
So go deep. Check in with yourself.
Who do you need to forgive?

3—SUNDAY

4—MONDAY

5—TUESDAY

6—WEDNESDAY

7—THURSDAY

8—FRIDAY

9—SATURDAY

*Clothe yourselves with tenderhearted mercy,
kindness, humility, gentleness, and patience.
Make allowance for each other's faults, and
forgive anyone who offends you. Remember,
the Lord forgave you, so you must forgive others.*
COLOSSIANS 3:12-13 NLT

OCTOBER 2021

Trust in God, the One who has loved you
and provided for you from the beginning,
and all else will fall into place.

10—SUNDAY

11—MONDAY   *Columbus Day*

12—TUESDAY

13—WEDNESDAY

14—THURSDAY

15—FRIDAY

16—SATURDAY

*Trust (lean on, rely on, and be confident) in the
Lord and do good; so shall you dwell in the
land and feed surely on His faithfulness,
and truly you shall be fed.*
PSALM 37:3 AMPC

OCTOBER 2021

As you begin to alleviate your stress by trusting
and delighting yourself in the Lord, committing
your way to Him, you will find yourself more still,
more at peace, more able to rest in God.

17—SUNDAY

18—MONDAY

19—TUESDAY

20—WEDNESDAY

21—THURSDAY

22—FRIDAY

23—SATURDAY

Be still and rest in the Lord; wait for Him and
patiently lean yourself upon Him; fret not yourself
because of him who prospers in his way.
PSALM 37:7 AMPC

OCTOBER 2021

Keep your eyes open for God's hand
in all circumstances. And praise Him
for the beauty of the ordinary, everyday
people and things that surround you.

24—SUNDAY

25—MONDAY

26—TUESDAY

27—WEDNESDAY

28—THURSDAY

29—FRIDAY

30—SATURDAY

This is the day that the LORD has made;
let us rejoice and be glad in it.
PSALM 118:24 ESV

NOVEMBER 2021

SUNDAY	MONDAY	TUESDAY	WEDNESDAY
31	1	2 *Election Day*	3
7 *Daylight Saving Time Ends*	8	9	10
14	15	16	17
21	22	23	24
28 *Hanukkah Begins at Sundown*	29	30	1

THURSDAY	FRIDAY	SATURDAY
4	5	6
11 *Veterans Day*	12	13
18	19	20
25 *Thanksgiving Day*	26	27
2	3	4

OCTOBER

S	M	T	W	T	F	S
					1	2
3	4	5	6	7	8	9
10	11	12	13	14	15	16
17	18	19	20	21	22	23
24	25	26	27	28	29	30
31						

DECEMBER

S	M	T	W	T	F	S
			1	2	3	4
5	6	7	8	9	10	11
12	13	14	15	16	17	18
19	20	21	22	23	24	25
26	27	28	29	30	31	

The Tower of Power

Some days there is nowhere to go but up. It's a fact. Not all moments in our day are going to be rosy. But thankfully, God has provided an exit plan for just such harrowing, stress-filled moments. When the going gets tough, get going to God. Shout His name and head for His presence. Run, climb, escape to Him—mentally, spiritually, emotionally, even physically if a church or chapel is nearby—a place of safety and strength, high above anything you are going through. With His presence surrounding you, nothing can really harm you. And you are given a space to catch your breath, calm your spirit, quiet your mind, settle your soul. Stay as long as you'd like until you're ready to face the challenge before you.

. . . .

I'm running to You, Lord, my Tower
of Power. For in You, I know I'm safe.

GOALS *for this* MONTH

- [ ] ....
- [ ] ....
- [ ] ....
- [ ] ....
- [ ] ....
- [ ] ....
- [ ] ....
- [ ] ....
- [ ] ....
- [ ] ....
- [ ] ....
- [ ] ....

*The name of the Lord is a strong tower;
the [consistently] righteous man [upright
and in right standing with God] runs into it
and is safe, high [above evil] and strong.*

PROVERBS 18:10 AMPC

OCTOBER-NOVEMBER 2021

What anxiety is weighing you down?
Give it to God; then stand tall.

31—SUNDAY *Halloween*

1—MONDAY

2—TUESDAY *Election Day*

3—WEDNESDAY

4—THURSDAY

5—FRIDAY

6—SATURDAY

Cast your burden on the Lord [releasing the weight of it] and He will sustain you; He will never allow the [consistently] righteous to be moved (made to slip, fall, or fail).

PSALM 55:22 AMPC

NOVEMBER 2021

Within God's story lies your own. Pray that He will give you the wisdom and knowledge you need to rise above your distress. Look for the secret He is aching to impart. Let Him show you the path to His light.

7—SUNDAY

Daylight Saving Time Ends

8—MONDAY

9—TUESDAY

10—WEDNESDAY

11—THURSDAY
Veterans Day

12—FRIDAY

13—SATURDAY

*The God of heaven. . .gives wisdom to the wise
and knowledge to those who have understanding!
He reveals the deep and secret things; He knows
what is in the darkness, and the light dwells with Him!*

DANIEL 2:19, 21-22 AMPC

NOVEMBER 2021

Never doubt that God has a plan
for your life and is working it out—
even this very moment.

14—SUNDAY

15—MONDAY

16—TUESDAY

17—WEDNESDAY

18—THURSDAY

19—FRIDAY

20—SATURDAY

*In my distress I cried out to the LORD; yes,
I prayed to my God for help. He heard me from
his sanctuary; my cry to him reached his ears. . . .
He reached down from heaven and rescued
me; he drew me out of deep waters.*

PSALM 18:6, 16 NLT

NOVEMBER 2021

Call. Pray. Listen. Then marvel at
the wonder of the knowledge of God.

21—SUNDAY

22—MONDAY

23—TUESDAY

24—WEDNESDAY

....
....
....
....

25—THURSDAY   *Thanksgiving Day*

....
....
....
....

26—FRIDAY

....
....
....
....

27—SATURDAY

....
....
....
....

*"This is GOD's Message, the God who made earth,
made it livable and lasting, known everywhere
as GOD: 'Call to me and I will answer you. I'll tell
you marvelous and wondrous things that you
could never figure out on your own.'"*

JEREMIAH 33:2-3 MSG

DECEMBER 2021

SUNDAY	MONDAY	TUESDAY	WEDNESDAY
28	29	30	1
5	6	7	8
12	13	14	15
19	20	21 *First Day of Winter*	22
26	27	28	29

THURSDAY	FRIDAY	SATURDAY
2	3	4
9	10	11
16	17	18
23	24 *Christmas Eve*	25 *Christmas Day*
30	31 *New Year's Eve*	1

NOVEMBER

S	M	T	W	T	F	S
	1	2	3	4	5	6
7	8	9	10	11	12	13
14	15	16	17	18	19	20
21	22	23	24	25	26	27
28	29	30				

JANUARY

S	M	T	W	T	F	S
						1
2	3	4	5	6	7	8
9	10	11	12	13	14	15
16	17	18	19	20	21	22
23	24	25	26	27	28	29
30	31					

Get Going

You had a plan. But things didn't turn out the way you thought they would. Yet you still seem to be sulking, brooding over what seems to be a lost opportunity, mourning what could've been, maybe even trying to force things to work out right.

God wants you to stop stressing over what could've been. He's ready for you to move on, to get going, to take the next step in His plan.

Ask God what His next move for you is. He has already spotted your next opportunity to cooperate with His plan and work out His good for all concerned. So what are you waiting for? Get going.

. . . .

I'm not sure, Lord, why things didn't
work out, but I know You have a plan.
So I'm ready, Lord. Where to?

GOALS *for this* MONTH

- [ ] ....
- [ ] ....
- [ ] ....
- [ ] ....
- [ ] ....
- [ ] ....
- [ ] ....
- [ ] ....
- [ ] ....
- [ ] ....
- [ ] ....
- [ ] ....

*GOD addressed Samuel: "So, how long are
you going to mope over Saul? You know I've
rejected him as king over Israel. Fill your flask
with anointing oil and get going. I'm sending
you to Jesse of Bethlehem. I've spotted the
very king I want among his sons."*

1 SAMUEL 16:1 MSG

NOVEMBER-DECEMBER 2021

Lean your entire self upon Christ,
and soon your stress will disappear
in the power of His love and light.

28—SUNDAY   *Hanukkah Begins at Sundown*

29—MONDAY

30—TUESDAY

1—WEDNESDAY

2—THURSDAY

3—FRIDAY

4—SATURDAY

We're depending on GOD; he's everything we need.
What's more, our hearts brim with joy since we've
taken for our own his holy name. Love us, GOD, with
all you've got—that's what we're depending on.

PSALM 33:20-22 MSG

DECEMBER 2021

When you have nothing but trouble, when stress is weighing you down, immobilizing you from doing anything for God, seek Him. You'll find Him waiting to hear your voice and to give you peace of mind, body, spirit, and soul.

5—SUNDAY

6—MONDAY

7—TUESDAY

8—WEDNESDAY

....

....

....

....

9—THURSDAY

....

....

....

....

10—FRIDAY

....

....

....

....

11—SATURDAY

....

....

....

....

If you seek Him [inquiring for and of Him,
craving Him as your soul's first necessity],
He will be found by you.

2 CHRONICLES 15:2 AMPC

DECEMBER 2021

Be the flower God has created you to be, the lily that has no worries for she knows her gardener is in her midst. And when you do, you will find yourself not stressed but blooming where you are planted.

12—SUNDAY

13—MONDAY

14—TUESDAY

15—WEDNESDAY

16—THURSDAY

17—FRIDAY

18—SATURDAY

*I, the Lord, am its Keeper; I water it
every moment; lest anyone harm it,
I guard and keep it night and day.*

ISAIAH 27:3 AMPC

DECEMBER 2021

God has given His people the freedom
and the power of choice. What will
you choose? Whom will you serve?

19—SUNDAY

20—MONDAY

21—TUESDAY

First Day of Winter

22—WEDNESDAY

23—THURSDAY

24—FRIDAY   *Christmas Eve*

25—SATURDAY   *Christmas Day*

*"Today I am giving you a choice between life
and death, between prosperity and disaster.
For I command you this day to love the LORD
your God and to keep his commands, decrees,
and regulations by walking in his ways."*

DEUTERONOMY 30:15-16 NLT

DECEMBER 2021-JANUARY 2022

God has given you life for a reason. He has a calling for you. Once you have made Jesus Lord of your life, it's time to be free, to be brave, to have peace in Him, and to be obedient to His voice. He wants you to take your stand and share His life with others.

26—SUNDAY

27—MONDAY

28—TUESDAY

29—WEDNESDAY

30—THURSDAY

31—FRIDAY   *New Year's Eve*

1—SATURDAY   *New Year's Day*

*During the night an angel of God opened the jailhouse
door and led them out. He said, "Go to the Temple
and take your stand. Tell the people. . .about this
Life." Promptly obedient, they entered the Temple
at daybreak and went on with their teaching.*

ACTS 5:19-20 MSG

CONTACTS

Name:

Address:

Phone: Cell:

Email:

Name:

Address:

Phone: Cell:

Email:

Name:

Address:

Phone: Cell:

Email:

Name:

Address:

Phone: Cell:

Email:

Name:

Address:

Phone: Cell:

Email:

CONTACTS

Name:

Address:

Phone: Cell:

Email:

Name:

Address:

Phone: Cell:

Email:

Name:

Address:

Phone: Cell:

Email:

Name:

Address:

Phone: Cell:

Email:

Name:

Address:

Phone: Cell:

Email:

CONTACTS

Name:

Address:

Phone: Cell:

Email:

Name:

Address:

Phone: Cell:

Email:

Name:

Address:

Phone: Cell:

Email:

Name:

Address:

Phone: Cell:

Email:

Name:

Address:

Phone: Cell:

Email:

CONTACTS

Name:

Address:

Phone: Cell:

Email:

Name:

Address:

Phone: Cell:

Email:

Name:

Address:

Phone: Cell:

Email:

Name:

Address:

Phone: Cell:

Email:

Name:

Address:

Phone: Cell:

Email:

CONTACTS

Name:

Address:

Phone: Cell:

Email:

Name:

Address:

Phone: Cell:

Email:

Name:

Address:

Phone: Cell:

Email:

Name:

Address:

Phone: Cell:

Email:

Name:

Address:

Phone: Cell:

Email:

CONTACTS

Name:

Address:

Phone: Cell:

Email:

Name:

Address:

Phone: Cell:

Email:

Name:

Address:

Phone: Cell:

Email:

Name:

Address:

Phone: Cell:

Email:

Name:

Address:

Phone: Cell:

Email:

CONTACTS

Name:

Address:

Phone: Cell:

Email:

Name:

Address:

Phone: Cell:

Email:

Name:

Address:

Phone: Cell:

Email:

Name:

Address:

Phone: Cell:

Email:

Name:

Address:

Phone: Cell:

Email:

CONTACTS

Name:

Address:

Phone: Cell:

Email:

Name:

Address:

Phone: Cell:

Email:

Name:

Address:

Phone: Cell:

Email:

Name:

Address:

Phone: Cell:

Email:

Name:

Address:

Phone: Cell:

Email:

CONTACTS

Name:

Address:

Phone: Cell:

Email:

Name:

Address:

Phone: Cell:

Email:

Name:

Address:

Phone: Cell:

Email:

Name:

Address:

Phone: Cell:

Email:

Name:

Address:

Phone: Cell:

Email:

CONTACTS

Name:

Address:

Phone: Cell:

Email:

Name:

Address:

Phone: Cell:

Email:

Name:

Address:

Phone: Cell:

Email:

Name:

Address:

Phone: Cell:

Email:

Name:

Address:

Phone: Cell:

Email:

CONTACTS

Name:

Address:

Phone: Cell:

Email:

Name:

Address:

Phone: Cell:

Email:

Name:

Address:

Phone: Cell:

Email:

Name:

Address:

Phone: Cell:

Email:

Name:

Address:

Phone: Cell:

Email:

CONTACTS

Name:

Address:

Phone: Cell:

Email:

Name:

Address:

Phone: Cell:

Email:

Name:

Address:

Phone: Cell:

Email:

Name:

Address:

Phone: Cell:

Email:

Name:

Address:

Phone: Cell:

Email:

CONTACTS

Name:

Address:

Phone: Cell:

Email:

Name:

Address:

Phone: Cell:

Email:

Name:

Address:

Phone: Cell:

Email:

Name:

Address:

Phone: Cell:

Email:

Name:

Address:

Phone: Cell:

Email:

CONTACTS

Name:

Address:

Phone: Cell:

Email:

Name:

Address:

Phone: Cell:

Email:

Name:

Address:

Phone: Cell:

Email:

Name:

Address:

Phone: Cell:

Email:

Name:

Address:

Phone: Cell:

Email:

2022

JANUARY

S	M	T	W	T	F	S
						1
2	3	4	5	6	7	8
9	10	11	12	13	14	15
16	17	18	19	20	21	22
23	24	25	26	27	28	29
30	31					

FEBRUARY

S	M	T	W	T	F	S
		1	2	3	4	5
6	7	8	9	10	11	12
13	14	15	16	17	18	19
20	21	22	23	24	25	26
27	28					

MARCH

S	M	T	W	T	F	S
		1	2	3	4	5
6	7	8	9	10	11	12
13	14	15	16	17	18	19
20	21	22	23	24	25	26
27	28	29	30	31		

APRIL

S	M	T	W	T	F	S
					1	2
3	4	5	6	7	8	9
10	11	12	13	14	15	16
17	18	19	20	21	22	23
24	25	26	27	28	29	30

MAY

S	M	T	W	T	F	S
1	2	3	4	5	6	7
8	9	10	11	12	13	14
15	16	17	18	19	20	21
22	23	24	25	26	27	28
29	30	31				

JUNE

S	M	T	W	T	F	S
			1	2	3	4
5	6	7	8	9	10	11
12	13	14	15	16	17	18
19	20	21	22	23	24	25
26	27	28	29	30		

JULY

S	M	T	W	T	F	S
					1	2
3	4	5	6	7	8	9
10	11	12	13	14	15	16
17	18	19	20	21	22	23
24	25	26	27	28	29	30
31						

AUGUST

S	M	T	W	T	F	S
	1	2	3	4	5	6
7	8	9	10	11	12	13
14	15	16	17	18	19	20
21	22	23	24	25	26	27
28	29	30	31			

SEPTEMBER

S	M	T	W	T	F	S
				1	2	3
4	5	6	7	8	9	10
11	12	13	14	15	16	17
18	19	20	21	22	23	24
25	26	27	28	29	30	

OCTOBER

S	M	T	W	T	F	S
						1
2	3	4	5	6	7	8
9	10	11	12	13	14	15
16	17	18	19	20	21	22
23	24	25	26	27	28	29
30	31					

NOVEMBER

S	M	T	W	T	F	S
		1	2	3	4	5
6	7	8	9	10	11	12
13	14	15	16	17	18	19
20	21	22	23	24	25	26
27	28	29	30			

DECEMBER

S	M	T	W	T	F	S
				1	2	3
4	5	6	7	8	9	10
11	12	13	14	15	16	17
18	19	20	21	22	23	24
25	26	27	28	29	30	31

2023

JANUARY

S	M	T	W	T	F	S
1	2	3	4	5	6	7
8	9	10	11	12	13	14
15	16	17	18	19	20	21
22	23	24	25	26	27	28
29	30	31				

FEBRUARY

S	M	T	W	T	F	S
			1	2	3	4
5	6	7	8	9	10	11
12	13	14	15	16	17	18
19	20	21	22	23	24	25
26	27	28				

MARCH

S	M	T	W	T	F	S
			1	2	3	4
5	6	7	8	9	10	11
12	13	14	15	16	17	18
19	20	21	22	23	24	25
26	27	28	29	30	31	

APRIL

S	M	T	W	T	F	S
						1
2	3	4	5	6	7	8
9	10	11	12	13	14	15
16	17	18	19	20	21	22
23	24	25	26	27	28	29
30						

MAY

S	M	T	W	T	F	S
	1	2	3	4	5	6
7	8	9	10	11	12	13
14	15	16	17	18	19	20
21	22	23	24	25	26	27
28	29	30	31			

JUNE

S	M	T	W	T	F	S
				1	2	3
4	5	6	7	8	9	10
11	12	13	14	15	16	17
18	19	20	21	22	23	24
25	26	27	28	29	30	

JULY

S	M	T	W	T	F	S
						1
2	3	4	5	6	7	8
9	10	11	12	13	14	15
16	17	18	19	20	21	22
23	24	25	26	27	28	29
30	31					

AUGUST

S	M	T	W	T	F	S
		1	2	3	4	5
6	7	8	9	10	11	12
13	14	15	16	17	18	19
20	21	22	23	24	25	26
27	28	29	30	31		

SEPTEMBER

S	M	T	W	T	F	S
					1	2
3	4	5	6	7	8	9
10	11	12	13	14	15	16
17	18	19	20	21	22	23
24	25	26	27	28	29	30

OCTOBER

S	M	T	W	T	F	S
1	2	3	4	5	6	7
8	9	10	11	12	13	14
15	16	17	18	19	20	21
22	23	24	25	26	27	28
29	30	31				

NOVEMBER

S	M	T	W	T	F	S
			1	2	3	4
5	6	7	8	9	10	11
12	13	14	15	16	17	18
19	20	21	22	23	24	25
26	27	28	29	30		

DECEMBER

S	M	T	W	T	F	S
					1	2
3	4	5	6	7	8	9
10	11	12	13	14	15	16
17	18	19	20	21	22	23
24	25	26	27	28	29	30
31